Healthy Snacks Cookbook

By CARLA HUTSON

Copyright 2024 By CARLA HUTSON. All rights reserved.

No part of this book may be reproduced in any form or by any electronic or mechanical means, including information storage and retrieval systems, without written permission from the author, except for the use of brief quotations in a book review.

Table of Contents

Chickpea Flour Pancakes 6

Baked Zucchini Chips 7

Watermelon Pizza 8

Spicy Roasted Chickpeas 9

Stuffed Mini Bell Peppers 10

Chocolate Banana Quinoa Bars 11

Cranberry Pistachio Energy Bars 12

Coconut Apricot Energy Bars 13

Avocado Toast with Egg 14

Greek Yogurt Parfait 15

Veggie Sticks with Hummus 16

Cottage Cheese with Pineapple 17

Almond Butter Apple Slices 18

Quinoa Salad Cups 19

Edamame Guacamole 20

Roasted Chickpeas 21

Banana Oat Cookies 22

Mango Salsa with Whole Grain Chips 23

Stuffed Bell Pepper Halves 24

Spinach and Feta Stuffed Mushrooms 25

Cucumber Roll-Ups with Hummus 26

Turkey and Cheese Lettuce Wraps 27

Fruit and Nut Butter Sandwiches 28

Greek Yogurt Bark 29

Sweet Potato Toast 30

Protein-Packed Egg Muffins 31

Crunchy Roasted Chickpeas 32

Apple Nachos	33
Cauliflower Popcorn	34
Cottage Cheese and Fruit Bowl	35
Chia Seed Energy Balls	36
Zucchini Pizza Bites	37
Tuna Salad Stuffed Avocado	38
Vegetable Sushi Rolls	39
Stuffed Bell Pepper Slices	40
Coconut Yogurt Parfait	41
Turkey and Veggie Roll-Ups	42
Mango Coconut Energy Balls	43
Cucumber Slices with Tzatziki	44
Hummus-Stuffed Mini Bell Peppers	45
Peanut Butter Banana Bites	46
Crispy Kale Chips	47
Cottage Cheese and Tomato Toast	48
Greek Yogurt Dip with Veggie Sticks	49
Egg Salad Lettuce Wraps	50
Chocolate Banana Protein Smoothie	51
Caprese Skewers	52
Tofu Veggie Spring Rolls	53
Cucumber Sushi Rolls	54
Chia Pudding	55
Apple Sandwiches with Peanut Butter and Granola	56
Mango Salsa with Baked Tortilla Chips	57
Veggie Stuffed Mini Peppers	58
Sweet Potato Toast with Almond Butter and Banana	59
Avocado Egg Salad	60

Coconut-Covered Strawberries 61

Mediterranean Chickpea Salad 62

Pumpkin Spice Energy Balls 64

Cauliflower Buffalo Bites 65

Watermelon Feta Skewers 66

Tuna Stuffed Avocado 67

Chickpea Flour Pancakes

Chickpea flour pancakes are a delicious and gluten-free alternative to traditional pancakes, perfect for a nutritious breakfast or snack.

TOTAL TIME COOKING: 15 minutes

Ingredients:

- 1 cup chickpea flour
- 1 cup water
- 1/2 teaspoon baking powder
- 1/4 teaspoon salt
- Optional add-ins: chopped vegetables, herbs, or spices

Directions:

1. In a mixing bowl, whisk the chickpea flour, water, baking powder, and salt until smooth.
2. Heat a non-stick skillet over medium heat and lightly grease with oil or cooking spray.
3. Pour a ladleful of batter onto the skillet and spread it into a round shape.
4. Cook for 2-3 minutes on each side until golden brown is cooked through.
5. Repeat with the remaining batter.
6. Serve these chickpea flour pancakes plain or with your favorite toppings for a delicious gluten-free snack!

Baked Zucchini Chips

These crispy baked zucchini chips are a healthier alternative to potato chips, seasoned with herbs and spices, for a flavorful gluten-free snack.

TOTAL TIME COOKING: 30 minutes

Ingredients:

- Zucchini, thinly sliced
- Olive oil
- Garlic powder
- Onion powder
- Paprika
- Salt and pepper to taste

Directions:

1. Preheat the oven to 425°F (220°C) and line a baking sheet with parchment paper.
2. toss thinly sliced zucchini with olive oil, garlic powder, onion powder, paprika, salt, and pepper until evenly coated.
3. Arrange the zucchini slices on the prepared baking sheet in a single layer.
4. Bake for 15-20 minutes, flipping halfway through, until the zucchini chips are golden and crispy.
5. Let cool before serving.
6. Enjoy these baked zucchini chips as a crunchy, flavorful, gluten-free snack!

Watermelon Pizza

Watermelon pizza is a refreshing and creative snack option that features watermelon slices topped with yogurt, fresh fruit, and nuts or seeds.

TOTAL TIME COOKING: 10 minutes

Ingredients:

- Watermelon, sliced into rounds or triangles
- Greek yogurt or coconut yogurt
- Assorted fresh fruit (such as berries, kiwi, mango, pineapple)
- Chopped nuts or seeds (such as almonds, walnuts, pumpkin seeds, chia seeds)
- Honey or maple syrup (optional)

Directions:

1. Spread a Greek or coconut yogurt layer onto each watermelon slice.
2. Top with assorted fresh fruit and chopped nuts or seeds.
3. Optional: Drizzle with honey or maple syrup for added sweetness.
4. Enjoy this watermelon pizza as a fun and nutritious snack or dessert!

Spicy Roasted Chickpeas

These spicy roasted chickpeas are a crunchy and satisfying snack with a kick of flavor, perfect for munching on the go.

TOTAL TIME COOKING: 40 minutes

Ingredients:

- Canned chickpeas (garbanzo beans), drained and rinsed
- Olive oil
- Smoked paprika
- Cayenne pepper
- Ground cumin
- Garlic powder
- Salt and pepper to taste

Directions:

1. Preheat the oven to 400°F (200°C) and line a baking sheet with parchment paper.
2. Pat the chickpeas dry with a paper towel and spread them on the prepared baking sheet.
3. Drizzle with olive oil and sprinkle with smoked paprika, cayenne pepper, ground cumin, garlic powder, salt, and pepper.
4. Toss the chickpeas until evenly coated.
5. Roast in the oven for 30-35 minutes, shaking the pan occasionally, until chickpeas are crispy.
6. Let cool before serving. Enjoy these spicy roasted chickpeas as a flavorful and addictive snack!

Stuffed Mini Bell Peppers

These stuffed mini bell peppers are filled with a savory mixture of quinoa, black beans, corn, and spices, creating a delicious and nutritious snack.

TOTAL TIME COOKING: 25 minutes

Ingredients:

- Mini bell peppers, halved and seeded
- Cooked quinoa
- Black beans, drained and rinsed
- Corn kernels (fresh or frozen)
- Salsa
- Cumin
- Chili powder
- Salt and pepper to taste
- Shredded cheese (optional)

Directions:

1. Preheat the oven to 375°F (190°C) and line a baking sheet with parchment paper.
2. Mix cooked quinoa, black beans, corn kernels, salsa, cumin, chili powder, salt, and pepper in a bowl.
3. Spoon the quinoa mixture into each mini bell pepper half.
4. Optional: Sprinkle with shredded cheese.
5. Place the stuffed mini bell peppers on the prepared baking sheet.
6. Bake for 15-20 minutes until the peppers are tender and the filling is heated through.
7. Enjoy these stuffed mini bell peppers as a flavorful and satisfying snack!

Chocolate Banana Quinoa Bars

These bars combine the goodness of quinoa, bananas, and chocolate for a delicious and nutritious snack.

TOTAL TIME COOKING: 25 minutes

Ingredients:

- 1 cup cooked quinoa
- 2 ripe bananas, mashed
- 1/4 cup honey or maple syrup
- 1/4 cup cocoa powder
- 1/4 cup almond butter
- 1/4 cup chopped nuts (optional)

Directions:

1. Preheat oven to 350°F (175°C) and grease a baking dish.
2. combine cooked quinoa, mashed bananas, honey or maple syrup, cocoa powder, almond butter, and chopped nuts in a mixing bowl.
3. Spread the mixture evenly into the prepared baking dish.
4. Bake for 15-20 minutes or until set.
5. Let cool before cutting into bars.

Cranberry Pistachio Energy Bars

These vibrant bars contain antioxidants and crunch, perfect for an on-the-go snack.

TOTAL TIME COOKING: 25 minutes

Ingredients:

- 1 1/2 cups rolled oats
- 1 cup dried cranberries
- 1/2 cup pistachios, chopped
- 1/4 cup honey
- 1/4 cup almond butter
- 1/4 teaspoon cinnamon

Directions:

1. In a food processor, pulse rolled oats until coarsely ground.
2. Add dried cranberries, chopped pistachios, honey, almond butter, and cinnamon. Process until the mixture sticks together.
3. Press the mixture firmly into a lined baking dish.
4. Refrigerate for 1 hour before slicing into bars.

Coconut Apricot Energy B

These tropical-inspired bars are a perfect blend of sweet a...

TOTAL TIME COOKING: 20 minutes

Ingredients:

- 1 cup dried apricots
- 1 cup shredded coconut
- 1/2 cup almonds
- 1/4 cup honey or maple syrup
- 1/4 teaspoon almond extract

Directions:

1. In a food processor, pulse-dried apricots until finely chopped.
2. Add shredded coconut, almonds, honey or maple syrup, and almond extract. Process until the mixture sticks together.
3. Press the mixture into a lined baking dish.
4. Refrigerate for 30 minutes, then cut into bars.

Avocado Toast with Egg

A nutritious and satisfying snack that balances healthy fats, protein, and carbohydrates.

TOTAL TIME COOKING: 10 minutes

Ingredients:

- 1 ripe avocado
- 2 slices whole grain bread
- 2 eggs
- Salt and pepper to taste
- Optional toppings: cherry tomatoes, microgreens, or feta cheese

Directions:

1. Toast the whole grain bread slices to your desired level of crispiness.
2. While the bread is toasting, mash the ripe avocado in a bowl and season with salt and pepper.
3. In a separate skillet, fry the eggs to your liking (sunny side up, over easy, etc.).
4. Spread the mashed avocado evenly on the toasted bread slices.
5. Top each slice with a fried egg and any optional toppings.
6. Sprinkle with additional salt and pepper if desired, and enjoy!

Greek Yogurt Parfait

A refreshing and protein-packed snack that can be customized with your favorite fruits and toppings.

TOTAL TIME COOKING: 5 minutes

Ingredients:

- 1 cup Greek yogurt
- 1/2 cup mixed berries (strawberries, blueberries, raspberries)
- 1/4 cup granola
- 1 tablespoon honey or maple syrup (optional)

Directions:

1. layer Greek yogurt, mixed berries, and granola in a glass or bowl.
2. Drizzle with honey or maple syrup if desired.
3. Repeat the layers until you reach the top of the glass or bowl.
4. Serve immediately and enjoy this delicious and nutritious parfait!

Veggie Sticks with Hummus

A crunchy and fiber-rich snack paired with creamy and protein-packed hummus.

TOTAL TIME COOKING: 10 minutes

Ingredients:

- Assorted veggies (carrots, cucumbers, bell peppers, celery)
- Store-bought or homemade hummus

Directions:

1. Wash and cut the assorted veggies into sticks or slices.
2. Arrange the veggie sticks on a plate or in a container.
3. Serve with hummus for dipping.
4. Enjoy this healthy and satisfying snack anytime!

Cottage Cheese with Pineapple

A high-protein snack that combines cottage cheese's creaminess with pineapple's sweetness.

TOTAL TIME COOKING: 5 minutes

Ingredients:

- 1/2 cup cottage cheese
- 1/2 cup fresh pineapple chunks

Directions:

1. Place cottage cheese in a bowl.
2. Top with fresh pineapple chunks.
3. Stir gently to combine, or enjoy each ingredient separately.
4. Serve immediately and savor the creamy and sweet flavors!

Almond Butter Apple Slices

A simple yet satisfying snack that perfectly balances crunch and creaminess.

TOTAL TIME COOKING: 5 minutes

Ingredients:

- 1 apple, sliced
- 2 tablespoons almond butter
- Optional toppings: cinnamon, honey, or granola

Directions:

1. Slice the apple into thin rounds or wedges, removing the core and seeds.
2. Spread almond butter on each apple slice.
3. Sprinkle with optional toppings such as cinnamon, honey, or granola.
4. Enjoy this delicious and nutritious snack that's perfect for any time of day!

Quinoa Salad Cups

These bite-sized quinoa salad cups are packed with protein and veggies, perfect for a quick and nutritious snack.

TOTAL TIME COOKING: 20 minutes

Ingredients:

- 1 cup cooked quinoa
- 1/2 cup diced cucumber
- 1/2 cup cherry tomatoes, halved
- 1/4 cup diced bell peppers
- 2 tablespoons chopped fresh herbs (such as parsley or cilantro)
- 2 tablespoons olive oil
- 1 tablespoon lemon juice
- Salt and pepper to taste

Directions:

1. combine cooked quinoa, diced cucumber, cherry tomatoes, bell peppers, and chopped fresh herbs in a mixing bowl.
2. Drizzle with olive oil and lemon juice, and season with salt and pepper. Mix well to combine.
3. Spoon the quinoa salad into small cups or containers.
4. Serve immediately or refrigerate until ready to eat.

Edamame Guacamole

A twist on traditional guacamole, this version is made with creamy avocado and protein-rich edamame.

TOTAL TIME COOKING: 15 minutes

Ingredients:

- 1 ripe avocado
- 1 cup cooked edamame, shelled
- 1/4 cup diced red onion
- 1/4 cup diced tomatoes
- 1 clove garlic, minced
- 1 tablespoon lime juice
- Salt and pepper to taste
- Optional toppings: chopped cilantro, diced jalapeño

Directions:

1. In a bowl, mash the ripe avocado until smooth.
2. Stir in cooked edamame, diced red onion, diced tomatoes, minced garlic, and lime juice.
3. Season with salt and pepper to taste.
4. Garnish with optional toppings if desired.
5. Serve with whole grain tortilla chips or veggie sticks for dipping.

Roasted Chickpeas

These crispy roasted chickpeas are a flavorful and satisfy with protein and fiber.

TOTAL TIME COOKING: 40 minutes

Ingredients:

- 1 can (15 oz) chickpeas (garbanzo beans), drained and rinsed
- 1 tablespoon olive oil
- 1 teaspoon ground cumin
- 1/2 teaspoon paprika
- 1/2 teaspoon garlic powder
- Salt to taste

Directions:

1. Preheat the oven to 400°F (200°C).
2. Pat the chickpeas dry with a paper towel and remove any loose skins.
3. toss the chickpeas with olive oil, ground cumin, paprika, garlic powder, and salt until evenly coated.
4. Spread the chickpeas in a single layer on a baking sheet lined with parchment paper.
5. Roast in the oven for 30-35 minutes, shaking the pan halfway through, until the chickpeas are crispy and golden brown.
6. Let cool before serving.

Banana Oat Cookies

These soft and chewy cookies are made with wholesome ingredients like bananas, oats, and nuts.

TOTAL TIME COOKING: 15 minutes

Ingredients:

- 2 ripe bananas, mashed
- 1 cup rolled oats
- 1/4 cup chopped nuts (such as walnuts or almonds)
- 1/4 cup raisins or dried cranberries
- 1 teaspoon cinnamon
- Optional add-ins: chocolate chips, shredded coconut

Directions:

1. Preheat the oven to 350°F (175°C) and line a baking sheet with parchment paper.
2. combine mashed bananas, rolled oats, chopped nuts, raisins or dried cranberries, and cinnamon in a mixing bowl.
3. Stir in any optional add-ins if desired.
4. Drop spoonfuls of the mixture onto the prepared baking sheet and flatten slightly with the back of a spoon.
5. Bake for 10-12 minutes or until golden brown.
6. Let them cool before enjoying these delicious and guilt-free cookies!

Mango Salsa with Whole Grain Chips

This vibrant mango salsa paired with whole-grain chips makes for a refreshing and nutritious snack.

TOTAL TIME COOKING: 15 minutes

Ingredients:

- 1 ripe mango, diced
- 1/2 cup diced red bell pepper
- 1/4 cup diced red onion
- 1/4 cup chopped fresh cilantro
- Juice of 1 lime
- Salt and pepper to taste
- Whole grain tortilla chips

Directions:

1. In a bowl, combine diced mango, red bell pepper, red onion, chopped fresh cilantro, and lime juice.
2. Season with salt and pepper to taste.
3. Serve the mango salsa with whole-grain tortilla chips for dipping.
4. Enjoy this sweet and savory snack that's bursting with flavor!

Stuffed Bell Pepper Halves

These colorful bell pepper halves are filled with a tasty mixture of hummus and crunchy veggies.

TOTAL TIME COOKING: 15 minutes

Ingredients:

- Bell peppers (assorted colors)
- Hummus (store-bought or homemade)
- Assorted veggies (such as cucumber, carrots, cherry tomatoes)
- Fresh herbs (such as parsley or dill) for garnish

Directions:

1. Slice bell peppers in half lengthwise and remove the seeds and membranes.

2. Fill each bell pepper half with a spoonful of hummus.

3. Top with assorted veggies of your choice.

4. Garnish with fresh herbs.

5. Serve immediately and enjoy these colorful and nutritious stuffed pepper halves!

Spinach and Feta Stuffed Mushrooms

These savory stuffed mushrooms are filled with a flavorful mixture of spinach, feta cheese, and herbs.

TOTAL TIME COOKING: 25 minutes

Ingredients:

- Large mushrooms, stems removed
- 1 cup spinach, chopped
- 1/4 cup crumbled feta cheese
- 1 clove garlic, minced
- 1 tablespoon olive oil
- Salt and pepper to taste

Directions:

1. Preheat the oven to 375°F (190°C) and line a baking sheet with parchment paper.

2. In a skillet, heat olive oil over medium heat. Add minced garlic and chopped spinach, and sauté until spinach is wilted.

3. Remove from heat and stir in crumbled feta cheese. Season with salt and pepper to taste.

4. Stuff each mushroom cap with the spinach and feta mixture.

5. Place stuffed mushrooms on the prepared baking sheet and bake for 15-20 minutes or until mushrooms are tender.

6. Serve warm and enjoy these delicious and nutritious stuffed mushrooms!

Cucumber Roll-Ups with Hummus

These light and refreshing cucumber roll-ups are filled with creamy hummus and crunchy veggies.

TOTAL TIME COOKING: 10 minutes

Ingredients:

- English cucumber
- Hummus (store-bought or homemade)
- Assorted veggies (such as bell peppers, carrots, avocado)
- Fresh herbs (such as parsley or cilantro)

Directions:

1. Using a vegetable peeler or mandoline, slice the cucumber lengthwise into thin strips.

2. Spread a thin layer of hummus onto each cucumber strip.

3. Place assorted veggies on top of the hummus.

4. Roll up the cucumber strips and secure them with toothpicks if needed.

5. Garnish with fresh herbs and serve these delightful cucumber roll-ups as a healthy snack or appetizer.

Turkey and Cheese Lettuce Wraps

These protein-packed lettuce wraps are a low-carb alternative to traditional sandwiches, perfect for a quick and satisfying snack.

TOTAL TIME COOKING: 10 minutes

Ingredients:

- Large lettuce leaves (such as romaine or butter lettuce)
- Sliced turkey breast
- Sliced cheese (such as cheddar or Swiss)
- Mustard or mayonnaise (optional)
- Sliced tomato, avocado, or cucumber (optional)

Directions:

1. Lay a lettuce leaf flat and top with sliced turkey breast and cheese.

2. Add mustard or mayonnaise, if desired, and any additional toppings of your choice.

3. Roll up the lettuce leaf to form a wrap.

4. Secure with toothpicks if needed, and enjoy these delicious and protein-rich lettuce wraps!

Fruit and Nut Butter Sandwiches

These mini sandwiches are made with slices of your favorite fruits and spread with creamy nut butter for a healthy and satisfying snack.

TOTAL TIME COOKING: 5 minutes

Ingredients:

- Sliced fruit (such as apples, bananas, or strawberries)
- Nut butter (such as almond butter or peanut butter)
- Whole grain bread or rice cakes

Directions:

1. Spread nut butter onto one slice of whole-grain bread or rice cake.

2. Top with sliced fruit and another slice of bread or rice cake to form a sandwich.

3. Cut into smaller pieces if desired, and enjoy these tasty and nutritious fruit and nut butter sandwiches!

Greek Yogurt Bark

This frozen treat is made with Greek yogurt and topped with your favorite fruits, nuts, and seeds for a refreshing and nutritious snack.

TOTAL TIME COOKING: 2 hours (including freezing time)

Ingredients:

- Greek yogurt (plain or flavored)
- Assorted fruits (such as berries, kiwi, or mango)
- Nuts (such as almonds, walnuts, or pistachios)
- Seeds (such as chia seeds or pumpkin seeds)
- Honey or maple syrup (optional)

Directions:

1. Line a baking sheet with parchment paper.

2. Spread Greek yogurt evenly onto the parchment paper, about 1/4 inch thick.

3. Top with sliced fruits, nuts, and seeds, and drizzle with honey or maple syrup if desired.

4. Place the baking sheet in the freezer for at least 2 hours or until the yogurt is frozen.

5. Once frozen, break the yogurt bark into pieces and enjoy this refreshing and nutritious frozen snack!

Sweet Potato Toast

Swap out traditional bread for roasted sweet potato slices to create a delicious and nutritious base for your favorite toppings.

TOTAL TIME COOKING: 25 minutes

Ingredients:

- Large sweet potatoes
- Assorted toppings (such as avocado, hummus, smoked salmon, cherry tomatoes, or almond butter)
- Optional seasonings (such as cinnamon, sea salt, or black pepper)

Directions:

1. Preheat the oven to 400°F (200°C) and line a baking sheet with parchment paper.

2. Slice the sweet potatoes lengthwise into 1/4-inch thick slices.

3. Place the sweet potato slices on the prepared baking sheet and bake for 20-25 minutes or until tender.

4. Once the sweet potato slices are cooked, top them with your favorite toppings and seasonings.

5. Enjoy these sweet and savory sweet potato toasts as a satisfying snack or light meal!

Protein-Packed Egg Muffins

These portable egg muffins are loaded with protein and veggies, making them the perfect grab-and-go snack or breakfast option.

TOTAL TIME COOKING: 30 minutes

Ingredients:

- Eggs
- Assorted veggies (such as spinach, bell peppers, onions, or mushrooms)
- Cheese (such as cheddar or feta)
- Salt and pepper to taste

Directions:

1. Preheat the oven to 350°F (175°C) and grease a muffin tin with cooking spray.

2. whisk together eggs, chopped veggies, cheese, salt, and pepper in a mixing bowl.

3. Pour the egg mixture into the prepared muffin tin, filling each cup about 3/4 full.

4. Bake for 20-25 minutes or until the egg muffins are set and golden brown.

5. Let it cool slightly before removing it from the muffin tin. Enjoy these protein-packed egg muffins, warm or cold!

Crunchy Roasted Chickpeas

These crispy roasted chickpeas are a flavorful and satisfying snack high in fiber and protein.

TOTAL TIME COOKING: 40 minutes

Ingredients:

- Canned chickpeas (garbanzo beans), drained and rinsed
- Olive oil
- Seasonings (such as paprika, garlic powder, cumin, or chili powder)
- Salt to taste

Directions:

1. Preheat the oven to 400°F (200°C) and line a baking sheet with parchment paper.

2. Pat the chickpeas dry with a paper towel and remove any loose skins.

3. In a bowl, toss the chickpeas with olive oil and your choice of seasonings until evenly coated.

4. Spread the seasoned chickpeas in a single layer on the prepared baking sheet.

5. Bake for 30-35 minutes, shaking the pan occasionally, until the chickpeas are crispy and golden brown.

6. Let cool before enjoying these crunchy roasted chickpeas as a delicious and nutritious snack!

Apple Nachos

These fun and easy apple nachos are a healthy twist on traditional nachos, featuring sliced apples topped with delicious and nutritious toppings.

TOTAL TIME COOKING: 10 minutes

Ingredients:

- Apples, cored and thinly sliced
- Nut butter (such as almond butter or peanut butter)
- Greek yogurt or coconut yogurt
- Toppings (such as granola, sliced almonds, shredded coconut, chocolate chips, or dried fruit)

Directions:

1. Arrange the sliced apples on a serving platter or plate.
2. Drizzle with nut butter and Greek yogurt.
3. Sprinkle with your favorite toppings, such as granola, sliced almonds, shredded coconut, chocolate chips, or dried fruit.
4. Serve immediately and enjoy these delicious and nutritious apple nachos as a fun and satisfying snack!

Cauliflower Popcorn

Enjoy the popcorn crunch with a healthier twist by making roasted cauliflower bites seasoned to perfection.

TOTAL TIME COOKING: 30 minutes

Ingredients:

- Cauliflower florets
- Olive oil
- Seasonings (such as nutritional yeast, garlic powder, onion powder, paprika, or sea salt)

Directions:

1. Preheat the oven to 425°F (220°C) and line a baking sheet with parchment paper.

2. Toss cauliflower florets with olive oil and your choice of seasonings until evenly coated.

3. Spread the seasoned cauliflower in a single layer on the prepared baking sheet.

4. Bake for 20-25 minutes or until the cauliflower is golden brown and crispy.

5. Let cool slightly before serving. Enjoy these flavorful cauliflower popcorn bites as a guilt-free snack!

Cottage Cheese and Fruit Bowl

A simple yet satisfying snack combining creamy cottage cheese with your favorite fresh fruits.

TOTAL TIME COOKING: 5 minutes

Ingredients:

- Cottage cheese
- Assorted fresh fruits (such as berries, sliced peaches, or pineapple chunks)
- Optional toppings: honey, cinnamon, or chopped nuts

Directions:

1. Spoon cottage cheese into a bowl.

2. Top with your choice of fresh fruits.

3. Drizzle with honey, sprinkle with cinnamon, or add chopped nuts if desired.

4. Enjoy this protein-rich and refreshing snack!

Chia Seed Energy Balls

These no-bake energy balls contain nutrient-dense ingredients like chia seeds, oats, and nut butter.

TOTAL TIME COOKING: 15 minutes

Ingredients:

- 1/2 cup rolled oats
- 1/4 cup chia seeds
- 1/4 cup nut butter (such as almond butter or peanut butter)
- 1/4 cup honey or maple syrup
- 1/4 cup shredded coconut
- Optional add-ins: chocolate chips, dried fruit, or protein powder

Directions:

1. combine rolled oats, chia seeds, nut butter, honey or maple syrup, and shredded coconut in a mixing bowl.

2. Stir in any optional add-ins if desired.

3. Roll the mixture into small balls using your hands.

4. Place the energy balls on a baking sheet lined with parchment paper and refrigerate for at least 1 hour before serving.

5. Enjoy these nutritious and portable energy balls as a quick snack on the go!

Zucchini Pizza Bites

These bite-sized zucchini pizza bites are a healthier alternative to traditional pizza snacks.

TOTAL TIME COOKING: 20 minutes

Ingredients:

- Zucchini, sliced into rounds
- Pizza sauce
- Shredded mozzarella cheese
- Mini pepperoni slices (optional)
- Italian seasoning

Directions:

1. Preheat the oven to 400°F (200°C) and line a baking sheet with parchment paper.

2. Place zucchini rounds on the prepared baking sheet.

3. Top each zucchini round with pizza sauce, shredded mozzarella cheese, and mini pepperoni slices if using.

4. Sprinkle with Italian seasoning.

5. Bake for 12-15 minutes or until the cheese is melted and bubbly.

6. Let cool slightly before serving. Enjoy these tasty zucchini pizza bites as a fun and nutritious snack!

Tuna Salad Stuffed Avocado

Creamy avocado halves filled with flavorful tuna salad make for a satisfying and protein-rich snack.

TOTAL TIME COOKING: 10 minutes

Ingredients:

- Ripe avocados, halved and pitted
- Canned tuna, drained
- Greek yogurt or mayonnaise
- Diced celery
- Diced red onion
- Lemon juice
- Salt and pepper to taste

Directions:

1. mix canned tuna, Greek yogurt or mayonnaise, diced celery, red onion, and lemon juice in a bowl.

2. Season with salt and pepper to taste.

3. Spoon the tuna salad mixture into the avocado halves.

4. Serve immediately and enjoy this delicious and nutritious tuna salad stuffed with avocados!

Vegetable Sushi Rolls

These homemade sushi rolls are filled with crisp vegetables and wrapped in nori sheets for a healthy and flavorful snack.

TOTAL TIME COOKING: 30 minutes

Ingredients:

- Sushi rice
- Nori sheets
- Assorted vegetables (such as cucumber, avocado, carrot, and bell pepper)
- Rice vinegar
- Soy sauce for dipping

Directions:

1. Cook sushi rice according to package instructions and season with vinegar.

2. Place a nori sheet on a bamboo sushi mat or clean kitchen towel.

3. Spread a thin layer of sushi rice evenly over the nori sheet, leaving a border along the edges.

4. Arrange thinly sliced vegetables in a row across the rice.

5. Roll up the sushi tightly using the bamboo mat or towel, sealing the edge with water.

6. Slice the sushi roll into bite-sized pieces using a sharp knife.

7. Serve these homemade vegetable sushi rolls with soy sauce for dipping and enjoy them as a healthy and satisfying snack!

Stuffed Bell Pepper Slices

These colorful bell pepper slices are filled with a flavorful mixture of hummus, veggies, and herbs.

TOTAL TIME COOKING: 15 minutes

Ingredients:

- Bell peppers (assorted colors)
- Hummus (store-bought or homemade)
- Assorted veggies (such as cucumber, cherry tomatoes, carrots)
- Fresh herbs (such as parsley or cilantro)
- Optional toppings: black olives, feta cheese

Directions:

1. Slice bell peppers into rings, removing the seeds and membranes.
2. Spread a layer of hummus inside each bell pepper ring.
3. Top with assorted veggies and fresh herbs.
4. Add optional toppings like black olives or feta cheese.
5. Serve these stuffed bell pepper slices as a colorful and nutritious snack!

Coconut Yogurt Parfait

This dairy-free yogurt parfait is made with creamy coconut yogurt and layered with fresh fruit and crunchy granola.

TOTAL TIME COOKING: 5 minutes

Ingredients:

- Coconut yogurt (store-bought or homemade)
- Fresh fruit (such as berries, mango, or kiwi)
- Granola
- Optional toppings: shredded coconut, chia seeds, or honey

Directions:

1. layer coconut yogurt, fresh fruit, and granola in a glass or jar.
2. Repeat the layers until the glass or jar is filled.
3. Top with optional toppings like shredded coconut or chia seeds.
4. Serve this coconut yogurt parfait immediately as a delicious and refreshing snack!

Turkey and Veggie Roll-Ups

These protein-packed roll-ups are filled with lean turkey breast and crunchy veggies, perfect for a quick and satisfying snack.

TOTAL TIME COOKING: 10 minutes

Ingredients:

- Sliced turkey breast
- Assorted veggies (such as bell peppers, cucumber, or carrots)
- Hummus or cream cheese

Directions:

1. Lay a slice of turkey breast flat on a clean surface.
2. Spread a thin layer of hummus or cream cheese on top.
3. Place sliced veggies on one end of the turkey slice.
4. Roll up the turkey slice tightly, enclosing the veggies.
5. Secure with toothpicks if needed and slice into bite-sized pieces.
6. Enjoy these turkey and veggie roll-ups as a nutritious, portable snack!

Mango Coconut Energy Balls

These tropical-inspired energy balls are made with dried mango, coconut, nuts, and seeds for a tasty and energizing snack.

TOTAL TIME COOKING: 15 minutes

Ingredients:

- Dried mango
- Shredded coconut
- Almonds or cashews
- Chia seeds
- Honey or maple syrup

Directions:

1. combine dried mango, shredded coconut, almonds or cashews, chia seeds, and honey or maple syrup in a food processor.

2. Pulse until the mixture comes together and forms a sticky dough.

3. Roll the mixture into small balls using your hands.

4. Optional: Roll the balls in additional shredded coconut for extra flavor.

5. Refrigerate the energy balls for at least 30 minutes before serving.

6. Enjoy these mango coconut energy balls as a delicious and nutritious snack!

Cucumber Slices with Tzatziki

These refreshing cucumber slices are served with creamy tzatziki sauce for a light and flavorful snack.

TOTAL TIME COOKING: 10 minutes

Ingredients:

- Cucumber, thinly sliced
- Tzatziki sauce (store-bought or homemade)
- Fresh dill or mint for garnish

Directions:

1. Arrange cucumber slices on a serving platter.
2. Spoon tzatziki sauce onto each cucumber slice.
3. Garnish with fresh dill or mint.
4. Serve these cucumber slices with tzatziki sauce as a refreshing and healthy snack!

Hummus-Stuffed Mini Bell Peppers

These bite-sized bell peppers are filled with creamy hummus, creating a flavorful and nutritious snack.

TOTAL TIME COOKING: 15 minutes

Ingredients:

- Mini bell peppers, halved and seeded
- Hummus (store-bought or homemade)
- Optional toppings: chopped fresh herbs, paprika, sesame seeds

Directions:

1. Fill each mini bell pepper half with hummus.

2. Sprinkle with optional toppings like chopped fresh herbs, paprika, or sesame seeds for extra flavor.

3. Arrange the stuffed bell pepper halves on a serving platter.

4. Serve these hummus-stuffed mini bell peppers as a delicious snack!

Peanut Butter Banana Bites

These simple yet delicious banana bites are topped with peanut butter and your favorite toppings for a sweet and satisfying snack.

TOTAL TIME COOKING: 10 minutes

Ingredients:

- Bananas, sliced into rounds
- Peanut butter (or any nut or seed butter)
- Toppings: shredded coconut, chopped nuts, chocolate chips, chia seeds

Directions:

1. Spread a thin peanut butter layer on each banana round.

2. Sprinkle with your favorite toppings, such as shredded coconut, chopped nuts, chocolate chips, or chia seeds.

3. Arrange the peanut butter banana bites on a plate.

4. Enjoy these tasty and nutritious bites as a satisfying snack or dessert option!

Crispy Kale Chips

These homemade kale chips are seasoned with spices and roasted until crispy for a healthy and addictive snack.

TOTAL TIME COOKING: 20 minutes

Ingredients:

- Fresh kale, washed and dried
- Olive oil
- Salt and pepper
- Optional seasonings: garlic powder, paprika, nutritional yeast

Directions:

1. Preheat the oven to 275°F (135°C) and line a baking sheet with parchment paper.

2. Tear the kale leaves into bite-sized pieces, removing the tough stems.

3. toss the kale with olive oil, salt, pepper, and any optional seasonings until evenly coated.

4. Spread the seasoned kale in a single layer on the prepared baking sheet.

5. Bake for 15-20 minutes or until the kale is crispy but not burnt.

6. Let cool before serving. Enjoy these crispy kale chips as a nutritious alternative to potato chips!

Cottage Cheese and Tomato Toast

This savory toast is topped with creamy cottage cheese, sliced tomatoes, and fresh herbs for a satisfying and protein-rich snack.

TOTAL TIME COOKING: 10 minutes

Ingredients:

- Whole grain bread, toasted
- Cottage cheese
- Sliced tomatoes
- Fresh basil leaves
- Olive oil
- Salt and pepper

Directions:

1. Spread a layer of cottage cheese on each slice of toasted whole-grain bread.

2. Arrange sliced tomatoes on top of the cottage cheese.

3. Drizzle with olive oil and season with salt and pepper to taste.

4. Garnish with fresh basil leaves.

5. Serve this cottage cheese and tomato toast as a delicious, satisfying snack or light meal!

Greek Yogurt Dip with Veggie Sticks

This creamy Greek yogurt dip paired with fresh veggie sticks makes for a healthy and delicious snack.

TOTAL TIME COOKING: 10 minutes

Ingredients:

- Greek yogurt
- Lemon juice
- Garlic, minced
- Fresh dill or parsley, chopped
- Assorted vegetable sticks (such as carrots, celery, bell peppers)

Directions:

1. mix Greek yogurt, lemon juice, minced garlic, and chopped fresh herbs in a bowl.

2. Season with salt and pepper to taste.

3. Serve the Greek yogurt dip with assorted vegetable sticks for dipping.

4. Enjoy this refreshing and nutritious snack any time of the day!

Egg Salad Lettuce Wraps

These egg salad lettuce wraps are light, refreshing, and protein-packed, making them a perfect snack or light lunch option.

TOTAL TIME COOKING: 15 minutes

Ingredients:

- Hard-boiled eggs, chopped
- Greek yogurt or mayonnaise
- Dijon mustard
- Dill pickles, chopped
- Green onions, chopped
- Lettuce leaves

Directions:

1. mix chopped hard-boiled eggs, Greek yogurt or mayonnaise, Dijon mustard, chopped dill pickles, and green onions in a bowl.

2. Season with salt and pepper to taste.

3. Spoon the egg salad mixture onto lettuce leaves.

4. Roll up the lettuce leaves to form wraps.

5. Enjoy these egg salad lettuce wraps as a healthy and satisfying snack!

Chocolate Banana Protein Smoothie

This creamy and indulgent smoothie is packed with protein, fiber, and antioxidants, making it a perfect post-workout snack or midday pick-me-up.

TOTAL TIME COOKING: 5 minutes

Ingredients:

- Ripe banana
- Protein powder (chocolate-flavored)
- Unsweetened almond milk or Greek yogurt
- Spinach leaves (optional)
- Ice cubes

Directions:

1. combine ripe banana, chocolate protein powder, unsweetened almond milk or Greek yogurt, spinach leaves (if using), and ice cubes.

2. Blend until smooth and creamy.

3. Pour the smoothie into glasses and enjoy it immediately as a delicious and satisfying snack!

Caprese Skewers

These colorful skewers are a delightful combination of fresh mozzarella, cherry tomatoes, and basil, drizzled with balsamic glaze.

TOTAL TIME COOKING: 10 minutes

Ingredients:

- Fresh mozzarella balls (bocconcini)
- Cherry tomatoes
- Fresh basil leaves
- Balsamic glaze
- Wooden skewers

Directions:

1. Thread a cherry tomato, a basil leaf, and a mozzarella ball onto each skewer.

2. Arrange the skewers on a serving platter.

3. Drizzle with balsamic glaze just before serving.

4. Enjoy these colorful and flavorful caprese skewers as a light and refreshing snack!

Tofu Veggie Spring Rolls

These refreshing spring rolls are filled with crispy tofu, crunchy vegetables, and fresh herbs and served with a delicious dipping sauce.

TOTAL TIME COOKING: 30 minutes

Ingredients:

- Rice paper wrappers
- Firm tofu, sliced into strips and baked until crispy
- Assorted vegetables (such as carrots, cucumber, bell peppers, lettuce)
- Fresh herbs (such as mint, cilantro, or basil)
- Dipping sauce (such as peanut sauce or sweet chili sauce)

Directions:

1. Dip a rice paper wrapper into warm water for a few seconds until soft and pliable.

2. Place the softened rice paper wrapper on a clean surface.

3. Layer crispy tofu strips, sliced vegetables, and fresh herbs on the bottom third of the rice paper wrapper.

4. Fold the sides of the wrapper over the filling, then roll up tightly.

5. Repeat with the remaining ingredients.

6. Serve the tofu veggie spring rolls with your favorite dipping sauce, and enjoy this light and nutritious snack!

Cucumber Sushi Rolls

These cucumber sushi rolls are a refreshing and low-carb alternative to traditional sushi rolls, filled with crisp vegetables and creamy avocado.

TOTAL TIME COOKING: 15 minutes

Ingredients:

- Large English cucumber
- Avocado, sliced
- Carrot, julienned
- Cucumber strips
- Bell pepper strips
- Alfalfa sprouts or microgreens
- Soy sauce or tamari for dipping

Directions:

1. A vegetable peeler slices the cucumber lengthwise into thin strips.

2. Lay the cucumber strips flat and layer with avocado slices, julienned carrot, cucumber strips, bell pepper strips, and alfalfa sprouts or microgreens.

3. Roll up the cucumber strips tightly to form sushi rolls.

4. Slice the rolls into bite-sized pieces.

5. Serve these light and refreshing cucumber sushi rolls with soy sauce or tamari for dipping and enjoy them!

Chia Pudding

This creamy chia pudding is made with chia seeds, almond milk, and natural sweeteners, topped with fresh fruit and nuts for a nutritious snack or breakfast option.

TOTAL TIME COOKING: 4 hours (including chilling time)

Ingredients:

- Chia seeds
- Almond milk (or any milk of your choice)
- Maple syrup or honey
- Vanilla extract
- Fresh fruit (such as berries, sliced banana, or mango)
- Chopped nuts (such as almonds, walnuts, or pecans)

Directions:

1. whisk together chia seeds, almond milk, maple syrup or honey, and vanilla extract in a bowl.

2. Cover and refrigerate for at least 4 hours or overnight until the mixture thickens and sets.

3. Stir the chia pudding well before serving.

4. Top with fresh fruit and chopped nuts before enjoying this creamy and satisfying chia pudding!

Apple Sandwiches with Peanut Butter and Granola

These apple sandwiches are a fun and delicious snack, filled with creamy peanut butter and crunchy granola for a satisfying combination of flavors and textures.

TOTAL TIME COOKING: 5 minutes

Ingredients:

- Apples, cored and sliced horizontally into rounds
- Peanut butter (or any nut or seed butter)
- Granola
- Optional toppings: raisins, shredded coconut, chocolate chips

Directions:

1. Spread peanut butter on one apple slice.

2. Sprinkle granola (optional toppings, if desired) over the peanut butter.

3. Top with another apple slice to form a sandwich.

4. Repeat with the remaining apple slices.

5. Enjoy these apple sandwiches as a tasty and nutritious snack or dessert!

Mango Salsa with Baked Tortilla Chips

This vibrant mango salsa is a refreshing and flavorful snack, served with homemade baked tortilla chips for dipping.

TOTAL TIME COOKING: 25 minutes

Ingredients:

- Ripe mango, diced
- Red onion, finely chopped
- Red bell pepper, diced
- Jalapeno pepper, seeded and minced
- Fresh cilantro, chopped
- Lime juice
- Salt and pepper to taste
- Corn tortillas

Directions:

1. combine diced mango, red onion, bell pepper, jalapeno pepper, and chopped cilantro in a bowl.

2. Drizzle with lime juice and season with salt and pepper to taste. Mix well.

3. Preheat the oven to 350°F (175°C).

4. Cut corn tortillas into triangles and arrange them in a single layer on a baking sheet.

5. Bake for 10-12 minutes or until the tortilla chips are crisp and golden brown.

6. Serve the mango salsa with the baked tortilla chips and enjoy this refreshing and flavorful snack!

Veggie Stuffed Mini Peppers

These colorful mini peppers are stuffed with a flavorful mixture of cream cheese, herbs, and vegetables, making them a tasty and healthy snack or appetizer.

TOTAL TIME COOKING: 20 minutes

Ingredients:

- Mini sweet peppers, halved and seeded
- Cream cheese (or goat cheese)
- Fresh herbs (such as chives, parsley, or dill), chopped
- Assorted finely chopped vegetables (such as cucumber, cherry tomatoes, or olives)
- Salt and pepper to taste

Directions:

1. mix cream cheese and chopped fresh herbs together in a bowl until well combined.

2. Stir in the chopped vegetables and season with salt and pepper to taste.

3. Spoon the cream cheese mixture into each halved mini pepper.

4. Arrange the stuffed mini peppers on a serving platter.

5. Enjoy these veggie-stuffed mini peppers as a colorful and flavorful snack or appetizer option!

Sweet Potato Toast with Almond Butter and Banana

This sweet potato toast is a nutritious and satisfying alternative to traditional bread, topped with creamy almond butter and sliced banana.

TOTAL TIME COOKING: 15 minutes

Ingredients:

- Sweet potatoes, sliced lengthwise into thin slices
- Almond butter
- Ripe banana, sliced

Directions:

1. Preheat the oven to 400°F (200°C) and line a baking sheet with parchment paper.

2. Place sweet potato slices on the prepared baking sheet and bake for 10-12 minutes or until tender.

3. Spread almond butter on each sweet potato slice.

4. Top with sliced banana.

5. Enjoy this delicious and nutritious sweet potato toast as a satisfying snack or breakfast option!

Avocado Egg Salad

This creamy and protein-rich avocado egg salad is made with ripe, hard-boiled eggs and fresh herbs for a flavorful and filling snack.

TOTAL TIME COOKING: 15 minutes

Ingredients:

- Ripe avocado
- Hard-boiled eggs, chopped
- Greek yogurt or mayonnaise
- Dijon mustard
- Fresh dill or chives, chopped
- Salt and pepper to taste

Directions:

1. In a bowl, mash the ripe avocado until smooth.

2. Stir in chopped hard-boiled eggs, Greek yogurt or mayonnaise, Dijon mustard, and fresh herbs.

3. Season with salt and pepper to taste.

4. Serve this avocado egg salad on whole grain crackers or cucumber slices for a nutritious and satisfying snack!

Coconut-Covered Strawberries

These coconut-covered strawberries are a simple and delicious treat, combining the sweetness of strawberries with the tropical flavor of coconut.

TOTAL TIME COOKING: 15 minutes

Ingredients:

- Fresh strawberries, washed and dried
- Coconut yogurt or melted coconut butter
- Shredded coconut

Directions:

1. Dip each strawberry into coconut yogurt or melted coconut butter, ensuring it's coated evenly.

2. Roll the coated strawberry in shredded coconut until fully covered.

3. Place the coated strawberries on a plate or baking sheet lined with parchment paper.

4. Refrigerate for 10-15 minutes or until the coating is set.

5. Enjoy these coconut-covered strawberries as a healthy and delicious snack or dessert option!

Mediterranean Chickpea Salad

This Mediterranean-inspired chickpea salad is packed with protein and fiber, featuring chickpeas, cucumber, cherry tomatoes, feta cheese, and a tangy vinaigrette.

TOTAL TIME COOKING: 15 minutes

Ingredients:

- Canned chickpeas (garbanzo beans), drained and rinsed
- Cucumber, diced
- Cherry tomatoes, halved
- Red onion, thinly sliced
- Kalamata olives, pitted and halved
- Feta cheese, crumbled
- Fresh parsley, chopped
- Olive oil
- Lemon juice
- Dried oregano
- Salt and pepper to taste

Directions:

1. In a large bowl, combine chickpeas, diced cucumber, halved cherry tomatoes, sliced red onion, halved Kalamata olives, crumbled feta cheese, and chopped fresh parsley.

2. whisk together olive oil, lemon juice, dried oregano, salt, and pepper in a small bowl to make the vinaigrette.

3. Pour the vinaigrette over the chickpea salad and toss until well combined.

4. Serve this Mediterranean chickpea salad chilled as a refreshing and nutritious snack or side dish!

Pumpkin Spice Energy Balls

These pumpkin spice energy balls are packed with fall flavors and wholesome ingredients, perfect for a quick and satisfying snack.

TOTAL TIME COOKING: 15 minutes

Ingredients:

- Rolled oats
- Pumpkin puree
- Almond butter
- Maple syrup
- Pumpkin pie spice (or a combination of cinnamon, nutmeg, ginger, and cloves)
- Chopped nuts (such as pecans or walnuts)
- Shredded coconut (optional)

Directions:

1. In a large bowl, mix rolled oats, pumpkin puree, almond butter, maple syrup, pumpkin pie spice, and chopped nuts until well combined.
2. Roll the mixture into small balls using your hands.
3. Optional: Roll the balls in shredded coconut for added flavor and texture.
4. Refrigerate the energy balls for at least 30 minutes before serving.
5. Enjoy these pumpkin spice energy balls as a tasty and nutritious snack on the go!

Cauliflower Buffalo Bites

These crispy cauliflower bites are coated in spicy buffalo sauce and baked until golden brown, offering a healthier twist on traditional buffalo wings.

TOTAL TIME COOKING: 30 minutes

Ingredients:

- Cauliflower florets
- Olive oil
- Garlic powder
- Salt and pepper
- Buffalo sauce (store-bought or homemade)
- Ranch or blue cheese dressing for dipping

Directions:

1. Preheat the oven to 450°F (230°C) and line a baking sheet with parchment paper.

2. toss cauliflower florets with olive oil, garlic powder, salt, and pepper until evenly coated.

3. Arrange cauliflower florets on the prepared baking sheet in a single layer.

4. Bake for 20-25 minutes until cauliflower is golden and crispy.

5. Remove from the oven and toss cauliflower in buffalo sauce until coated.

6. Serve these cauliflower buffalo bites with ranch or blue cheese dressing for dipping.

Watermelon Feta Skewers

These refreshing skewers are a delightful combination of sweet watermelon, tangy feta cheese, and fresh mint, perfect for a light and flavorful snack.

TOTAL TIME COOKING: 15 minutes

Ingredients:

- Seedless watermelon, cut into cubes
- Feta cheese, cut into cubes
- Fresh mint leaves
- Balsamic glaze (optional)

Directions:

1. Thread a cube of watermelon, feta cheese, and a fresh mint leaf onto each skewer.

2. Arrange the skewers on a serving platter.

3. Drizzle with balsamic glaze, if desired, just before serving.

4. Enjoy these watermelon feta skewers as a refreshing and delicious snack or appetizer!

Tuna Stuffed Avocado

These tuna stuffed avocados are filled with a flavorful mixture of canned tuna, Greek yogurt, and crunchy vegetables, offering a protein-packed and satisfying snack.

TOTAL TIME COOKING: 10 minutes

Ingredients:

- Ripe avocados, halved and pitted
- Canned tuna, drained
- Greek yogurt
- Red onion, finely chopped
- Celery, finely chopped
- Lemon juice
- Salt and pepper to taste

Directions:

1. Mix canned tuna, Greek yogurt, chopped red onion, chopped celery, and lemon juice until well combined.

2. Season with salt and pepper to taste.

3. Spoon the tuna mixture into each avocado half.

4. Serve these tuna stuffed avocados as a nutritious and filling snack or light meal!

Printed in Great Britain
by Amazon